Goals and Goal Setting

Achieve measurable results

Fourth Edition

Larrie A. Rouillard

A Crisp Fifty-Minute™ Series Book

AXZO  PRESS

Goals and Goal Setting

Achieve measurable results

Fourth Edition

Larrie A. Rouillard

CREDITS:

President, Axzo Press:	**Jon Winder**
Vice President, Product Development:	**Charles G. Blum**
Vice President, Operations:	**Josh Pincus**
Director, Publishing Systems Development:	**Dan Quackenbush**
Copy Editor:	**Ken Maher**

ISBN 10: 1-4260-1835-5
ISBN 13: 978-1-4260-1835-0
Printed in the United States of America
2 3 4 5 6 7 8 9 10 13 12 11 10

Table of Contents

Appendix 85

About the Author

Larrie Rouillard is founder and president of Lar Corp of Oklahoma City, Oklahoma, a consulting company that specializes in helping business men and women succeed by improving their skills. Larrie conducts business skills assessments, identifies areas for operational improvement, works with individuals who need specific skill development, and conducts classes on goal setting, negotiating, and strategic planning.

Larrie has developed, marketed, and delivered over 20 skill-building training curricula focused on core skills needed most in today's business world, including oral and written presentation, negotiation, listening, problem-solving, decision-making, goal setting, and time management.

Larrie can be contacted at:

Lar Corp
8700 South Council Road
Oklahoma City, OK 73169
(405) 745-5002
Fax (405) 745-3740

Email: Lar_corp@msn.com

Dedication

To Tina, my purpose and my strength; to Richard and Carolyn, my guides and role models; and to Travis and Brian—may they find an honorable life mission and make their mark through goal achievement.

Preface

I'm often asked why I chose to write a book goals and goal setting.

The truth is, it didn't start out as my idea. A former boss realized that most of our staff didn't know how to formally and effectively set and achieve business goals, so he assigned me the task of creating a fundamental, easy-to-use, and repeatable goal-setting structure for our organization. This book evolved from my original, 20-plus-page training manual based on his idea.

Looking back, I realize that many of the goals we set out to achieve don't start with our own ideas. Instead, they arise from tasks dictated by someone else—a family member, boss, customer, or client. But while a certain goal may not start out as our idea, how we adopt and adapt it as our own is often critical to its achievement.

This edition of *Goals and Goal Setting* builds on and refines some of the ancillary elements of the goal-setting process, such as discovering and managing obstacles. There is an expanded section on the positive effects of visualization on motivation and execution. I've also provided updated examples that are more in line with current thinking on the goal-setting and achievement process.

Today there are even more goal-setting resources on the Web to draw upon and utilize to help formulate, track, manage, and achieve goals: articles, worksheets, and video clips on the general topic of goals, as well as specific elements of the goal-setting process. While some of these resources offer different perspectives or even definitions from my own, they nevertheless reinforce the overall principles, purpose, and power of utilizing a goal-setting process to achieve your goals.

If you're a fan of the previous editions, I hope you'll find the new additions helpful. And for all readers, I hope my book helps you to set and achieve goals that bring security, prosperity, and happiness!

Larrie G. Rouillard

Larrie Rouillard

Why Goals and Goal Setting?

A sense of accomplishment is one of the more satisfying pleasures a person can experience. Beating the competition to market with a new product, landing that big account after months of hard work, or finally getting rid of a nasty habit—these are all things that people delight in achieving.

To be successful, you have to work hard, be a problem solver, and use your creativity and imagination to develop new products and ideas. Each achievement along the way doesn't happen by accident—it is one outcome of a larger pattern of successes. Careful planning, thoughtful strategy, and faithful and consistent execution are all factors that contribute to establishing such patterns. Through their focus and determination, they make success a self-fulfilling prophecy.

Before you take action, however, you have to have a goal. A goal can be personal or professional, individual or team-oriented. It is the point that you or your team must reach. Setting a goal that truly motivates isn't as easy as it sounds, but it's certainly not too difficult to be worth your while. A goal's extraordinary power over the success of your business or personal life is what makes goal setting essential.

This book addresses the important process of goal setting and achievement. Inside, you'll find activities that help you understand what a goal is, how to set realistic yet powerful goals, how to formulate an action plan, and how to achieve the goals you set. Step by step, you'll practice how to:

▶ Define and differentiate among goals, missions, and objectives.

▶ Follow a proven technique for establishing realistic yet powerful goals.

▶ Formulate and follow a Goal Action Plan.

▶ Execute the tactics needed to achieve your goals.

To learn any process well, you have to practice it. You'll have more success when you know the purposes of the process you want to learn. Discovering the purposes of goals and goal setting is the first step in learning these new skills.

The Purpose of Goal Setting

The first question you might ask about goal setting is, "What's in it for me?" To answer this question, we've separated the discussion to cover what a goal is and how to picture the process of setting and achieving organizational, business, and personal goals.

To begin to think about the purpose of goal setting, think of the questions journalists ask when writing a story:

What?	To identify goals.
Why?	To recognize that goal setting is essential to achieving success.
Who?	To understand the roles of the people involved in the goal-setting process.
Where?	To locate opportunities for useful goals.
How?	To understand a process that will help you reach you goals and what you want to achieve.

The only question missing is, "*When?*" You're the best person to answer that question.

Remember, these objectives are interrelated. When you understand them, you'll see that setting and achieving goals are essential to success in business as well as in the rest of life.

Which of the following might be goals in your life?

▶ Increasing sales and profits.

▶ Improving productivity in your department.

▶ Managing time more effectively.

▶ Seeing the Eiffel Tower in Paris.

▶ Capturing the business of an important client.

▶ Reducing operating expenses in a critical area in the organization.

▶ Being a vice-president of your company.

▶ Developing a new product within an allotted budget.

▶ Learning to play the piano.

▶ Gaining market share for your primary product.

If any of these are goals for you, or if you have similar goals, then you might ask yourself questions such as these:

▶ *Why can't I...?*

▶ *Why haven't I...?*

▶ *Why don't I...?*

The answer to each of these questions might be one of the following:

▶ You have no real desire to achieve that goal. If you lack desire, achieving a goal for its own sake won't motivate you enough. You also won't get the same sense of accomplishment if you do achieve the goal.

▶ You don't know how to establish motivating, stimulating, functional, and executable goals.

If you want to improve department productivity, develop that new product within budget, or see the Eiffel Tower, then you must learn how to set meaningful goals and establish executable objectives to help you reach those goals. Success at goal setting requires understanding a basic process for obtaining particular outcomes. That means goal identification, formulation, and execution.

Why Set Goals?

Goals are an essential part of successfully conducting business and living a rewarding life. Well-defined goals allow you to set and hit important targets (objectives) necessary to achieve the results (missions) you desire. Goals do the following:

▶ Establish **direction** for ongoing activities.

▶ Identify **expected results**.

▶ Improve **teamwork** through a common sense of purpose.

▶ Heighten performance by setting **targets** to be achieved.

Goals provide the motivation and direction necessary for growth and success in many important areas. In business, for example:

▶ If you never set goals, how will you know where you're headed?

▶ If no goals exist against which to measure progress, how do you know how you're doing?

▶ If there are no goals, how will you know when you succeed?

Question:

Would you get on an airplane if you didn't know where it was going to land?

Learning Objectives

Complete this book and you'll know how to:

1) Define the terms *mission, goal,* and *objective* and identify the elements of a well-written goal.

2) Discuss the roles of leaders and individuals in the goal-setting process and identify the benefits and drawbacks of top-down and bottom-up goal setting.

3) Identify opportunities for finding goals and document goals by using the S.M.A.R.T. method.

4) Develop a goal, create an action plan to achieve it, and overcome common obstacles along the way.

5) Implement, monitor, and revise a goal action plan to achieve a goal.

Workplace and Management Competencies mapping

For over 30 years, business and industry has utilized competency models to select employees. The trend to use competency-based approaches in education and training, assessment, and development of workers has experienced a more recent emergence within the Employment and Training Administration (ETA), a division of the United States Department of Labor.

The ETA's General Competency Model Framework spans a wide array of competencies from the more basic competencies, such as reading and writing, to more advanced occupation-specific competencies. The Crisp Series finds its home in what the ETA refers to as the Workplace Competencies and the Management Competencies.

Goals and Goal Setting covers information vital to mastering the following competencies:

Workplace Competencies:

▶ Adaptability & Flexibility

▶ Planning & Organizing

For a comprehensive mapping of Crisp Series titles to the Workplace and Management competencies, visit www.CrispSeries.com.

About the Crisp 50-Minute Series

The Crisp 50-Minute Series is designed to cover critical business and professional development topics in the shortest possible time. Our easy-to-read, easy-to-understand format can be used for self-study or for classroom training. With a wealth of hands-on exercises, the 50-Minute books keep you engaged and help you retain critical skills.

What You Need to Know

We designed the Crisp 50-Minute Series to be as self-explanatory as possible. But there are a few things you should know before you begin the book.

Exercises

Exercises look like this:

EXERCISE TITLE

Questions and other information will be here.

Keep a pencil handy. Any time you see an exercise, you should try to complete it. If the exercise has specific answers, an answer key is provided in the appendix. (Some exercises ask you to think about your own opinions or situation; these types of exercises don't have answer keys.)

Forms

A heading like this means that the rest of the page is a form:

FORMHEAD

Forms are meant to be reusable. You might want to make a photocopy of a form before you fill it out, so that you can use it again later.

A Note to Instructors

We've tried to make the Crisp 50-Minute Series books as useful as possible as classroom training manuals. Here are some of the features we provide for instructors:

- ▶ PowerPoint presentations
- ▶ Answer keys
- ▶ Assessments
- ▶ Customization

PowerPoint Presentations

You can download a PowerPoint presentation for this book from our Web site at www.CrispSeries.com.

Answer keys

If an exercise has specific answers, an answer key will be provided in the appendix. (Some exercises ask you to think about your own opinions or situation; these types of exercises will not have answer keys.)

Assessments

For each 50-Minute Series book, we have developed a 35- to 50-item assessment. The assessment for this book is available at www.CrispSeries.com. *Assessments should not be used in any employee-selection process.*

Customization

Crisp books can be quickly and easily customized to meet your needs—from adding your logo to developing proprietary content. Crisp books are available in print and electronic form. For more information on customization, see www.CrispSeries.com.

What Is a Goal?

"Nothing happens unless first we dream."

—Carl Sandburg

In this part:

▶ Understanding goals.

▶ Understanding missions.

▶ Understanding objectives.

▶ The goals and objectives pyramids.

▶ Overview: what is a goal?

Goals

To understand goals, we first need a working definition:

Goal

*An **end** toward which you direct **specific effort**.*

The *end* must be an exact and tangible result toward which you're willing to expend effort. What kind of effort and how much of it is always related to the goal itself. That is, you must be able to identify and weigh the cost/benefit relationship. Planning and analyzing the steps involved in reaching your goal will help you to do so.

Elements of a Goal

▶ **An accomplishment to be achieved**

This element of a goal answers the question, "What do I expect the outcome of my (our) actions to be?" In most cases you want to express this outcome with an action verb. (We'll take a closer look at using action verbs in Part 3.) For example:

I want to reduce operating expense in my department from 2% of sales to 1.5%.

▶ **A measurable outcome**

This element answers the question, "How will I know when I've reached the outcome?" or "What are the signs I need to see so that I know I've reached the goal?" The situation surrounding the outcome has to include things you can use to determine that you've reached the goal—simple, identifiable signs of success. For example:

The operating expense was 2% in June, 1.9% in July, and now 1.65% in August. The expenses are heading in the right direction.

▶ **A specific date and time by which to accomplish the goal**

This element answers, "When do I want to complete the goal?" It's essential to specify the exact date and time by which you want to have accomplished your goal. For example:

Reduce business expenses not to exceed 1.5% of total sales for this calendar year.

▶ **A maximum cost (money, time, and resources)**

This element answers, "What is the maximum cost in money, time, and resources that I'll allow myself in order to achieve this goal?" The cost and resource constraint forces you to place a financial value on the outcome. For example:

This reduction in operating expense will be achieved with the current headcount and without lowering existing service standards.

These elements help to clarify our definition of a goal:

Goal

*A **specific** and **measurable** outcome to be achieved within a **specified time** and under **specific cost constraints**.*

Goals Must Be Written!

Writing goals down in black and white results in more explicit statements of intent. Daydreaming about your goals doesn't help you reach them. Writing your goals down strengthens your commitment.

Look at these written goals:

▶ *Increase* productivity in our division 5% by August 15, without adding any personnel.

▶ *Gain* five new customers and increase gross sales to $50,000 by July 1 within an expense budget of $5,000.

▶ *Expand* market share to 5% by December 31 without increasing advertising expenses beyond current levels.

▶ *Secure* two clients by June 30 to produce $50,000 incremental income and require only 30% of my time to service.

▶ *Retire* from work and relocate to a warm climate.

You might think the first and last statements have some fuzzy elements in them. Do they have all the elements they need to be considered goals under our current definition? What about the other three?

IDENTIFYING GOAL ELEMENTS

Identify the goal elements in each of the following statements:

1. Gain five new customers and increase gross sales to $50,000 by July 1 with an expense budget of $5,000.

   Action verb: _____

   _____

   Measurable outcome: _____

   _____

   Specific date: _____

   _____

   Cost or resource constraint: _____

   _____

2. Expand market share to 5% by December 31 without increasing advertising expense beyond current levels.

   Action verb: _____

   _____

   Measurable outcome: _____

   _____

   Specific date: _____

   _____

   Cost or resource constraint: _____

   _____

CONTINUED

3. Secure two clients by June 30 to produce $50,000 incremental income and require no more than 30% of my time to service.

Action verb: _____

_____

Measurable outcome: _____

_____

Specific date: _____

_____

Cost or resource constraint: _____

_____

*Compare your answers with the author's suggested responses
in the Appendix.*

PRACTICE WRITING A GOAL

With practice, you'll learn to recognize easily the elements of a goal. Now that you know what the elements are, try writing a simple goal that includes all these elements.

Action Verb: _____

_____

_____

_____

Measurable Outcome: _____

_____

_____

_____

Specific Date: _____

_____

_____

_____

Cost or Resource Constraint: _____

_____

_____

_____

_____

_____

_____

Missions

One of the purposes of this book is to help you distinguish missions, goals, and objectives from each other. Knowing the differences among these three related types of statements will help you formulate better goals and achieve better, more lasting results. Here's a succinct look at the relationships among missions, goals, and objectives:

▶ **Missions** are general intents.

▶ **Goals** are specific and measurable accomplishments to be achieved.

▶ **Objectives** are tactics that you use to reach and achieve goals.

Mission

A general statement through which a person specifies the overall strategy or intent that governs that person's goals and objectives.

A mission statement provides the "reason for being." It enables you to clarify your purpose both for yourself and for others. Here are some examples of various types of mission statements:

Business: Be the recognized world leader in widget sales.

Athletic: Be a Super Bowl contender.

Personal: Travel in Europe.

A good mission statement should:

▶ State clearly the nature of your cause.

▶ Define your areas of concentration.

▶ Identify the markets you serve.

▶ Describe your organization's direction.

▶ Indicate your general plan for getting there.

Do you know any organization's mission statement? Write it here:

_____

_____

_____

_____

Formulating Missions

Formulating a mission is an essential part of the goal-setting process. A mission focuses direction and the efforts for reaching the goals and objectives that follow. An example of a personal mission is:

Be a role model and make a positive contribution to my community and country.

Any and all goals and objectives you develop must complement and contribute to the fulfillment of the mission. Some possible complementary goals for this mission might be:

▶ Get a medical degree from a leading institution.

▶ Earn an MD in cancer research by age 30.

▶ Specialize in a field that is actively pursuing an achievable cancer cure.

Effective goals complement the overall mission. If you had no mission and no sense of direction, it would be difficult to establish any meaningful goals. Here's another example of a mission:

Take an active leadership role in protecting our natural resources and environment.

What are some possible complementary goals for this mission? Write them here:

_____

_____

_____

A Comment about Missions

The creation of a mission statement requires careful thought and extensive planning. Every aspect of your personal or company life should be touched by the sense of purpose and direction described in the mission statement. Most importantly, the goals you establish and the work you perform must contribute to the fulfillment of the mission.

A well-prepared mission statement should reflect what the organization stands for—its employees and managers. It should also describe how we plan to treat or relate to those we live and work with. Ideally, the mission statement guides personal behavior and management style and directs how people are rewarded, trained, and developed.

Many organizations lack an effective mission statement. As a result, employees have no clear direction, sense of purpose, or loyalty. They have no desire to create unity and don't show commitment to organizational success. Without a mission statement for direction, goals tend to represent busywork rather than productive and profitable activity that moves the organization forward.

Objectives

"…And the cow jumped over the moon. But
not before getting the required permits."

You have examined the elements needed for goal statements and learned how
mission statements direct the goals you should set. The next step is to learn the role
that objectives play in the achievement of your goals.

Objectives

*Tactics that are **complementary** to a goal, just as goals must be
complementary to a mission.*

For example, consider the following mission and complementary goal:

Mission: Be a role model and make a positive contribution to the community.

Goals: Become a research scientist.

Some complementary objectives might be as follows. Notice that each objective is
broken down into more granular objectives (steps). These are the *tactics* you use to
achieve your goals.

Excel in high school studies.

1. Enroll in classes that support scientific study.

2. Focus on biology, chemistry, and mathematics.

Identify undergraduate and postgraduate institutions.

1. Determine an area of health care research interest.

2. Identify institutions that specialize in this chosen area.

3. Investigate potential institutions to narrow choices.

4. Visit likely candidate schools.

Apply to chosen undergraduate schools.

1. Complete application forms.

2. Solicit letters of recommendation from school, community, and work references.

3. Prepare for interviews.

Use undergraduate studies as postgraduate platform.

1. Choose courses in your area of interest.

2. Apply for a summer internship in a specific academic institution.

3. Identify a role model or mentor connected to health care research.

The objectives are the steps you take to reach your goal. They determine how quickly you reach your goal and the methods you use to do so.

Goals and Objectives Pyramids

A pyramid provides a good visualization of the relationship between mission, goals, and objectives. It can also help represent the varied approaches you use to achieve your goals.

The relationship between objectives and goals depends on the specific goal and your personal preference for how to reach it. There are many possible relationships between goals and objectives. Here are illustrations of some of those relationships:

▶ **Several objectives to achieve one goal**

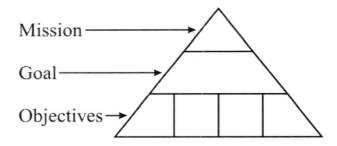

▶ **One objective to achieve one goal**

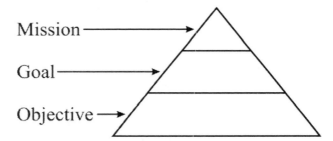

▶ **Several objectives to achieve several goals**

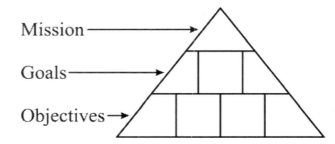

Choosing the approach that most appropriately fits your mission will help you to set and achieve your goals.

Overview: What Is a Goal?

Goal

An end toward which you direct specific effort.

The **elements of a goal** are:

► An accomplishment to be achieved

► A measurable outcome

► A specific date and time by which to accomplish the goal

► A maximum cost (in terms of money, time, and resources)

These elements lead to an expanded definition:

Goal

A specific and measurable accomplishment to be achieved within specified time, resource, and cost constraints.

A **written goal** provides a strong statement of your intent and the results to be achieved. Goal statements contain these elements:

► Action verbs

► Measurable outcomes

► Specific dates

► Cost or resource constraints

A **mission statement** describes the overall intent for an individual, organization, or business, as well as its reason for being. Goals must be complementary to the fulfillment of the stated mission.

Objectives are tactics used to accomplish goals. They must also be complementary to the goals of the mission.

Who Sets Goals?

> "Give me a stock clerk with a goal and I'll give you a man who will make history."

—J. C. Penney

In this part:

▶ Who sets goals is important.

▶ Understanding roles and responsibilities.

▶ The goal-setting process.

▶ The ownership issue.

▶ Adopting and adapting to a goal.

Who Sets Goals Is Important

Some goals are individual; they're achieved through the effort of a single person seeking to achieve a personal outcome. Others are team goals, those we achieve as part of a team or group dedicated to fulfilling a mission. Group and individual goals are set by people with different roles.

Who we are in relation to those others with a vested interest in the achievement of a goal is an important consideration. We each have roles and responsibilities to others (and ourselves) for goal setting and goal achievement.

Motivation

Who sets a goal is critical to its achievement, because it has a strong effect on **motivation**. Without personal commitment and effort, we can't achieve our goals. Both the person who sets the goals and those charged with the tasks leading to its achievement must be motivated to do what's necessary for goal success.

Motivation is the key to creating the commitment to do whatever is needed to reach the goal and fulfill the mission.

The Commitment Formula:

Individual + Motivation = Goal Commitment

Each individual responsible for goal achievement must find the personal motivation required to achieve the goal. Participation in the goal-setting process is the surest method of motivating individuals to commit to the goal's achievement. People are far more committed to reaching goals they help create.

Active participation in the goal-setting process includes being involved in all the elements of the goal's definition:

> ▶ Defining the accomplishment.

> ▶ Determining the specific, measurable outcomes.

> ▶ Creating the timeline of activities and deadlines for completion.

> ▶ Identifying the money, time, and other resources needed for goal achievement.

Active participation produces ownership, creating the desire and commitment that individuals need to work toward goal achievement.

Roles and Responsibilities

We all have roles to play, both in our public and private lives. Within these roles, we have specific responsibilities. The roles we play and the responsibilities our roles entail play an important part in the goal setting and achievement process, for ourselves and for the groups of which we are a part.

Roles

Each of us has various roles to play in life. There are two general role categories: public (our jobs, for example) and private (our family roles, for example).

Most of us have many public roles. For example, a middle manager in an organization may have the following roles to play:

▶ Subordinate (to managers above)

▶ Supervisor (to those below)

▶ Colleague (to peers)

▶ Mentor (to specific individuals within or outside the organization)

▶ Worker (for themselves or a supervisor)

▶ Stockholder (in the company)

We can have as many or more roles in our private world, including:

▶ Husband/wife

▶ Son/daughter

▶ Father/mother

▶ Leader/coach

▶ Host

▶ Spiritual advisor

▶ Friend/relative

Each of us can play multiple roles in both our public and private lives at the same time. That is, we can be husband/father/son/soccer coach at the same time we are associate/supervisor/colleague.

The roles we play allow us to identify potential goals.

Responsibilities

The roles we play point toward potential goals, because there are specific responsibilities associated with these roles. Responsibility means being able to answer for one's conduct and obligations. It implies taking action, when action is needed, and doing what's necessary to fulfill one's obligation to others, the organization, and oneself. Responsibilities provide abundant sources for goals.

One example of a private role/responsibility relationship might be:

Role	Responsibility	Goal Seed	Objective
Father	To raise well-educated children	Save enough money for a college education.	Buy savings bonds.
			Establish annuity.
			Spend less on leisure activities.

While a public example could be:

Role	Responsibility	Goal Seed	Objective
Supervisor	To provide direction to subordinates	Be available to help individuals solve problems.	Keep an open door.
			Hold weekly meetings
			Do quarterly reviews.

Note that a goal seed is only a starting point from which to identify a potential goal opportunity. Each seed needs to be further defined, developed, and completed within the formal goal-setting process.

WHAT ROLES DO YOU PLAY?

Name some of the roles you play in both the public and the private world. For each role you identify, write down a responsibility associated with it.

Private Role	**Responsibility**
_____	_____
_____	_____
_____	_____
_____	_____

Public Role	**Responsibility**
_____	_____
_____	_____
_____	_____

Now identify potential seeds for goals that arise from the role/responsibility relationships above.

1. _____

_____

2. _____

_____

3. _____

_____

4. _____

_____

The Goal Setting Process

The goal-setting process should be an individual one, but leaders must take an active role. The leader and individuals work together in a negotiation to set the goals to be achieved.

The Leader's Role

Leaders must guide, direct, and manage both the goal-setting and the goal-achievement processes. Goal setting should include negotiation between the people who are responsible for accomplishing the goal (the committed individuals) and those who would like to see the goals achieved (leadership). In this negotiation, leaders must ensure the following:

▶ The goal agreed to is complementary to the overall mission.

▶ All parties involved agree on all elements of the goals.

The Three-Step Process

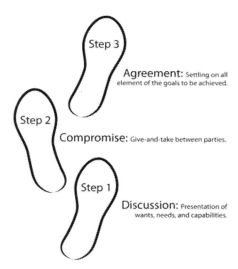

Successful agreement on goals involves a three-step process:

1. **Discussion**: Presentation of wants, needs, and capabilities

2. **Compromise**: Give-and-take between parties

3. **Agreement**: Settling on all elements of the goals to be achieved

Discussion

The discussion step involves getting all the interested parties together to discuss the "who, what, when, why, where, how, and how much" of the desired goal. In this step, open discussion is essential, so that everyone is assured that the intent and purpose of the goal is to fulfill the mission. Open discussion exposes areas of agreement and disagreement so that the parties can proceed to the next step: compromise.

Compromise

Before goals can be set, the parties must compromise on areas of disagreement. There must be give and take between the parties who will work to achieve the goal and those who are responsible for its achievement. Compromise establishes the goal boundaries, the elements of the goal to be executed, and the expected results to be accomplished. Compromise is the necessary path to agreement.

Agreement

Agreement closes out the compromise step and has all goal elements as its output. Everyone involved must agree on the accomplishment, the measurable outcome, the timeline, and the costs. It's also important to have agreement on the benefits of the goal's achievement (hard and soft), as well as on the methods to be used to achieve it. Without the agreement of everyone involved, the goal may not be reached. Therefore, the most essential element in the process of goal setting is communication.

Communication

Good communication is how you let other people know what's going on. Goals are difficult to achieve unless everyone clearly understands the mission and its associated goals.

Communication is crucial for:

▶ Clarifying goals and objectives

▶ Assigning responsibility

▶ Managing activities

▶ Measuring progress

The Ownership Issue

Who owns the goal can have a critical impact on its prospects for achievement. This makes it important to consider how the goal is established. There are two general approaches to goal setting:

▶ **Bottom-up goal setting**: Individuals at lower levels commit to what they can do to achieve the goal.

▶ **Top-down goal setting**: Management sets the goals for lower levels to achieve.

Each method has benefits and drawbacks.

Bottom-Up Goal Setting

Although it's frequently more time-consuming and difficult, bottom-up goal setting often creates stronger motivation, because it puts the responsibility where the goal achievement activities will occur (for example, where the product is made or where the services are provided). When all those who must contribute to goal *achievement* are involved in the goal *setting*, better results ensue because of higher individual commitment.

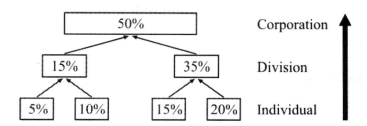

In the example above, the overall corporate goal is to create a 50% increase in revenue. Each individual commits to a share: 5%, 10%, 15%, and 20%, respectively. This commitment means that the two divisions contribute 15% and 35% shares to the goal of a 50% increase.

Top-Down Goal Setting

"I want productivity tripled withoiut the workers even knowing. Can you do it?"

When the goals to be achieved by lower levels are dictated by their leaders, we call this top-down goal setting. In this model, goals reflect the needs of the whole and are used to determine the specific contribution required at lower levels.

The expected results of the top-down goal-setting method can be the same as those of a bottom-up method. Note that the values in the example below are the same as those shown in the bottom-up example. On the surface, the only difference between the two examples appears to be the direction of the arrow.

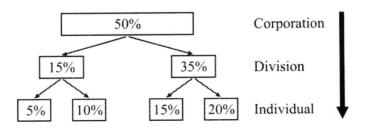

Top-down goal-setting often precludes the communication involved in the discussion, compromise, and agreement phases. The drawback of the top-down method is that active participation in the goal-setting process by *all* parties concerned helps to create the ownership and team effort necessary for successful goal achievement. Participant ownership produces the most critical factor for goal achievement: personal motivation.

WHAT HAPPENS IN YOUR ORGANIZATION?

Briefly describe how goals are set in your organization or department:

_____

_____

_____

_____

Does your organization rely on top-down or bottom-up goal setting?

❑ Top-down   ❑ Bottom-up

What are some advantages to the way your organization sets its goals?

_____

_____

_____

_____

What are some disadvantages?

_____

_____

_____

_____

How could the goal-setting procedures in your organization be improved?

_____

_____

_____

_____

Adopt and Adapt the Goal

Whether or not the goal is of your own choosing and whether you work independently or in a group, fulfillment of an assigned goal becomes your responsibility. In many goal-setting situations, you aren't the one setting the goal. Often, you'll be assigned a task and expected to achieve it. Here are some examples:

▶ Meeting a sales quota

▶ Reaching scholastic benchmarks (passing grades)

At other times, you won't have complete control over your assigned goal, such as would be the case when participating on a team to develop a new product. So how do you motivate yourself to achieve *someone else's goal?*

Regardless of how a goal is formulated: top-down, bottom-up, assigned, volunteered, or tasked, you must make the imposed goal manageable and relevant to you if you want to achieve it. Think of it this way:

1. Translate the goal into an individual goal; bring it down to your personal level.

2. **Adopt** the goal as your own.

3. **Adapt** the goal to a personal benefit

Adopt

You must adopt specific goal-achievement tasks—or the relevant parts of a team task—as your own by thinking, talking, and acting as if they were your own ideas. This helps create the positive vibes you need to follow through with your responsibilities. This approach is also helpful in team environments where positive group dynamics can increase both personal and team motivation.

Adapt

Then, you must adapt the goal to your own circumstances. That is, you need to find a way actually to make it your own. For example, don't focus on a quota you've been told to achieve. Concentrate instead on something more personal that will happen when that quota is met. Rather than focusing on passing grades, think about the prestige associated with graduating with honors. Or, imagine the reward that awaits you as a result of the successful outcome (that is, achievement of the goal).

Overview: Who Sets Goals?

In this part, you learned how being involved in the setting of goals affects motivation:

▶ Active **participation** in the goal-setting process creates **motivation**, which leads to **commitment** and success.

▶ Our **roles** in life carry **responsibilities**. Within our roles and responsibilities, we can often find seeds for possible goals.

▶ The goal-setting process involves **discussion**, **compromise**, and finally, **agreement**.

▶ **Ownership** is crucial to whether you achieve your goals. **Top-down goal-setting** creates little ownership but can be expedient. **Bottom-up goal-setting** creates much more ownership but can be costly and difficult to manage.

▶ Regardless of a goal's source, you must make it manageable and relevant to you, if you want to achieve it. To do this, start by translating the goal into an individual goal. You have to **adopt** the goal as your own and then **adapt** it to carry a personal benefit.

PART 3

Identifying and Documenting Goals

Goals are discovered, not made."

—Richard J. Foster

In this part:

▶ Goal identification and documentation.

▶ Task 1: Identifying goal opportunities.

▶ Task 2: Writing SMART goal statements.

▶ Overview: Writing SMART goal statements.

Goal Identification and Documentation

"Goals? Yes, I have goals! High score on this video game."

Goals can evolve from your wishes, hopes, and dreams, but most often they result from a discovery process that identifies your needs. Most of these needs arise from reviewing your roles and addressing the responsibilities they entail. Once you uncover the "who, what, when, how, and how much" of a particular need, you have the raw material for goal setting and goal achievement.

Goal setting is a sequence of events that enables the creation of attainable, actionable, and rewarding goals that lead to positive results. Identifying potential goals is a first step. Then your goals must be documented (written), creating a foundation for actions and achievement.

The initial two-task process looks like this:

> **Task 1**: Identify opportunities for goals
>
> **Task 2**: Write goal statements

Task 1:
Identifying Goal Opportunities

Questions: Where can I find potential goals?
Where can I find the best opportunities for creating goals?

Answer: All around you!

Goals can evolve from almost any aspect of your life so long as they contribute to the fulfillment of your mission. There's so much around us that we draw on to produce meaningful, worthwhile goals that it can be overwhelming. It's often helpful to focus on a smaller part of the universe. Because motivation is a key factor in goal achievement, you should seek goal opportunities in areas that contain built-in motivators.

Here are two categories on which to focus your search for goals:

▶ **Our needs**

▶ **Goal types**

Needs

Needs are perfect starting points for goals because they contain an abundant source of relevant and challenging opportunities. More importantly, a *need* motivates us to *act*.

Needs are a great source for goals, because we work harder to reach a goal that satisfies an unfulfilled need. That is, we willingly and purposefully direct our energies toward our most pressing needs.

Maslow's Hierarchy of Needs

Abraham Maslow identified a hierarchy of needs that recognized the strong motivational influence of human needs from the physiological to self-actualization. Maslow's hierarchy has physiological needs, those of basic survival, as its lowest level. Other levels include safety, love, worth, and finally self-actualization.

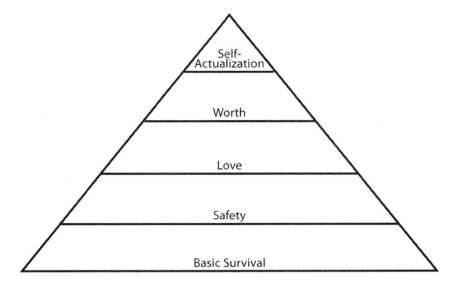

We can experience need at all five levels. Maslow argued, however, that our lower-level needs must be satisfied before we're motivated to direct our energy toward a higher-level need. That is, a person must satisfy his or her hunger (a basic survival need) before that person seeks out ways to be out of harm's way (a safety need).

Maslow's Needs in Our World

Maslow described the hierarchy, from high to low, as self-actualization, worth, love, safety, and survival. In our lives, we often see the hierarchy in the search for:

1. **Power** and **knowledge**. There's a need to control our own destinies. Power goals can include mastery over tasks or people. Knowledge goals are a manifestation of the universal desire to know and understand the world around us.

2. **Recognition** and **status**. People want to stand out from others. We often set goals whose achievement causes others to notice us.

3. **Achievement**. This is the desire to do something worthwhile for its own sake (altruistic motives).

4. **Security**. We seek to reduce the dangers around us.

5. **Money**. We want to increase our incomes. Therefore, we set goals that lead to greater wealth (a guarantee of survival).

The following illustration shows how these needs might map to one representation of Maslow's hierarchy.

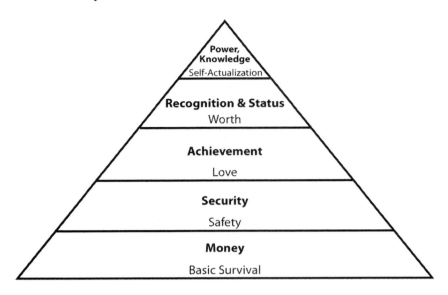

Each of these categories can provide direction for creating worthwhile goals for both our personal and public lives. For example, a desire to have enough money to take a special vacation might require setting and achieving a goal resulting in bonus compensation. Or you might use the desire to achieve recognition and status as motivation to achieve the same goal.

Using Needs to Build Goals

Using needs to stimulate goal ideas requires asking a series of questions:

> **Question**: What do I need?
>
> **Answer**: Money? Power? Knowledge? Achievement? Recognition? Security?
>
> **Question**: What do I need and what goals must be achieved to satisfy this need?
>
> **Answer**: Put this answer in the form of a specific goal statement.
>
> **Question**: What specific actions or tasks must be completed to achieve this goal?
>
> **Answer**: This answer will determine your objectives and help you to develop an action plan (see Part 4).

And finally:

> **Question**: How does the achievement of this goal fit in with my mission?
>
> **Answer**: Answering this question will ensure that your goal and its objectives are complementary to fulfilling the mission.

Career Needs

An example of a career needs statement might be: *I would like to have sufficient income to have my own resources, so I can quit relying on others for my success.*

Again, this one statement suggests many needs that you might then use as a basis for potential goals. For example:

► Sufficient income

► Additional resources

► Greater self-reliance

Each need can become the basis for a distinct goal statement:

► Increase sales by 5% per quarter for the year ending March 31 by developing new clients outside our current market while not adding additional salespeople.

► Purchase one new truck every six months beginning April 1, using increased sales to finance the cost, with cost not to exceed 1% of net sales increase.

CREATING GOALS BASED ON A NEED

Write down a need that you have in your personal or public life:

_____

_____

_____

Now try to write down potential goals that arise from this need:

1. _____

_____

2. _____

_____

3. _____

_____

4. _____

_____

Goal Types

Identifying goals by type clarifies their importance to the mission. There are three types of goals that differ in their contributions to the mission:

▶ **Essential goals** are required for the operation of the business or for personal improvement; they must be done.

▶ **Problem-solving goals** propose a more appropriate or desired condition, or ways around obstacles.

▶ **Innovative goals** result in something better, faster, cheaper, easier, or safer.

Understanding goal types helps uncover possible goal opportunities and can clarify a goal's relative importance. Let's investigate goal types in more detail.

Essential Goals

Essential goals identify everyday activities that must be fulfilled to ensure successful results. Essential goals are the recurring, ongoing, repetitious, and necessary activities for ongoing success. For example:

Review yesterday's results by 9:00 A.M. and correct errors before new work begins.

Can you think of an essential goal that you must accomplish on a regular basis? (Hint: Getting up on time tomorrow may be part of an essential goal, if it's to ensure you'll be on time for an important meeting.) Write it here.

_____

_____

Sources of essential goals are found within your roles and responsibilities. Therefore, assess these to uncover goals that must be achieved on a regular basis.

For example, if your area of responsibility is distributing the mail, then you must set goals for specific activities, such as efficient mail sorting, timing considerations, and effective delivery routes.

Problem-Solving Goals

A problem-solving goal identifies opportunities to create more appropriate, or desired, conditions. These goals may state the current situation but should include the desired, future situation after the goal is achieved.

Problem-solving goals outline actions that are necessary to improve performance. While they're vital for growth, they're probably not essential to survival. For example:

Reduce the number of mismatched invoices from 50% to 20% of those received by the end of the 4th quarter, with no additions to headcount.

This statement outlines the problem (50% of invoices received are currently mismatched) and the desired condition (20% mismatched). The desired condition is the outcome element of the goal.

Can you think of a problem-solving goal that you want to accomplish? Write it here:

_____

_____

_____

Sources for problem-solving goals are:

▶ Aspects of a task that can be improved, such as productivity, efficiency, accident prevention, and knowledge retention.

▶ Less-than-effective uses of time or resources.

▶ Obstacles that can be eliminated in the workplace.

Ask yourself, *"What's involved in solving these problems?"* The answer to this question can provide the seeds for developing problem-solving goals.

Innovative Goals

An innovative goal improves the current condition. Innovative goals don't involve solving problems but rather are the result of thinking about making something good even better. They identify activities to be done better or more quickly, cheaply, easily, or safely. For example:

> *Change the existing computer-buying system to reduce the number of hours needed to determine purchase quantities by the end of the 2nd quarter, using existing programs to keep development costs below $10,000.*

This goal says that, although there may be nothing *wrong* with the current system, improvements could be made in order to determine purchase quantities more easily. The *good* system would then be *better*.

Create an innovative goal and write it here.

_____

_____

_____

Other Potential Areas

Many other aspects of business or personal life can provide opportunities for goal creation. For example:

▶ **Profitability**. Increasing profitability may require essential, problem-solving, or innovative goals. Focus on profitability from three perspectives: cost, price, and expanded sales. All could yield more profit; therefore, profitability provides three sources for goals.

▶ **Self-improvement**. Self-improvement might mean finding additional areas of interest or new responsibilities within your personal or work life. These are goals you might want to accomplish within a year or two or longer. Setting essential or innovative goals can be great avenues to self-improvement.

▶ **Market conditions**. Analyze the needs of your market to create problem-solving or innovative goals. Analyze customer needs, uncover market weaknesses, and identify market advantages.

Identifying Goal Opportunities: Overview

▶ Goals can be anything, so long as they contribute to the mission of the individual, business, or organization.

▶ Goals identify the actions needed to reach our ultimate hopes, dreams, needs, and desires.

▶ Goals arise from needs, roles, and responsibilities. They can come from our business or our personal lives.

▶ Goals should not change once they're set. However, the objectives you set for reaching goals can and should change as conditions change.

▶ Essential goals must be accomplished for the success of the organization or the individual.

▶ Problem-solving goals ought to be achieved to correct ineffective conditions and thereby produce better results.

▶ Innovative goals are those you would like to accomplish in order to make something good even better (faster, cheaper, safer, or easier).

Essential goals shouldn't be passed over to achieve the relatively less important problem-solving or innovative goal types. Innovative or problem-solving goals shouldn't jeopardize your ability to achieve essential goals.

Try to find opportunities to achieve multiple goals by completing objectives that are common to two or more goals. Obviously, doing so requires careful planning and written goal statements that you can mix and match as needed.

Task 2:
Writing S.M.A.R.T. Goal Statements

A well-defined goal statement is the foundation for goal achievement. The goal is only as good as its clear statement of intent to:

- ▶ Fulfill one's responsibilities.

- ▶ Solve a problem.

- ▶ Be creative and innovative.

- ▶ Satisfy the personal or organizational mission.

A goal statement defines and formalizes:

- ▶ *What* is to be accomplished.

- ▶ *Who* will be involved.

- ▶ *When* the activity will be completed.

- ▶ *How* much it will cost and what resources will be used.

Using the S.M.A.R.T. method ensures that all these elements are included in a well-defined goal statement. The S.M.A.R.T. acronym's letters stand for the following qualities of a good goal statement:

S **pecific**

M **easurable**

A **ction-oriented**

R **ealistic**

T **ime- and resource-constrained**

A goal statement that demonstrates each of these qualities provides an excellent basis for setting and monitoring progress and achieving the goal.

S.M.A.R.T. Goals Are Specific

Specific means detailed, particular, and focused. A goal is specific when everyone knows exactly what's to be achieved and accomplished. Being specific means spelling out the details of the goal. For example, consider this goal statement:

Increase productivity.

It's too general, because it doesn't provide any specific information about what's to be accomplished. This example is somewhat better:

Increase staff productivity.

It does narrow the scope of the desired outcome, but it's still too general. To be most specific, the goal statement should say something like this:

Increase the data-entry output (productivity) of the staff.

This last statement specifies the specific output that you want to improve, leaving no doubt about what's to be accomplished. Specifying the expected end result is the first step toward creating a S.M.A.R.T. goal.

HOW SPECIFIC IS THE GOAL?

Rate the following statements by placing a check (✓) in the appropriate column. Are they specific enough to spell out the details of the desired goal? Why or why not?

	Too General	Not Specific Enough	More Specific
1. Wash and clean the car.	❏	❏	❏
2. Wash and clean the car each week.	❏	❏	❏
3. Wash and clean the car inside and out each week.	❏	❏	❏
4. Get better grades in school.	❏	❏	❏
5. Get better math grades in school.	❏	❏	❏
6. Get at least a B in math in school each semester.	❏	❏	❏
7. Study more often.	❏	❏	❏
8. Study my assignments every day.	❏	❏	❏
9. Study my math assignments at least one hour each day.	❏	❏	❏

Write an example of a *specific* outcome.

_____

_____

Compare your answers with the author's suggested responses in the Appendix.

S.M.A.R.T. Goals Are Measurable

Measurable goals are quantifiable. A measurable goal provides a standard for comparison, the means to an end, anda specific result; and it's limiting. Each goal must be measurable—it must have a method for comparison that indicates when the goal is reached. Doing something "better" or "more accurately" doesn't provide the quantifiable measurement necessary to determine goal achievement. These words are too ambiguous to use for a measurable outcome.

Consider this example:

> *Increase the data-entry output of the staff.*

It *is* a specific statement, but it's not measurable. This example is better:

> *Increase the data-entry output of the staff to 40 completed orders per day.*

The words "40 completed orders per day" provide a standard for comparison and monitoring progress. Counting the completed orders each day will indicate the progress made toward the goal and will determine when the 40-orders-per-day goal is reached.

WHICH ARE MEASURABLE OUTCOMES?

Circle **Y** (Yes) or **N** (No) to indicate whether each of the following is a measurable outcome. Remember that measurable outcomes must be quantifiable and limiting, providing a standard for comparison.

1. Provide better service to all my customers.　　　　　**Y　　N**

2. Answer every letter received within five work days.　　**Y　　N**

3. Significantly reduce the number of complaints.　　　　**Y　　N**

4. Lower the number of complaints by 50% from current levels.　**Y　　N**

5. Add only very productive individuals to the staff.　　**Y　　N**

Write a *measurable* outcome here.

_____

_____

_____

Compare your answers with the author's suggested responses
in the Appendix.

S.M.A.R.T. Goals Are Action-Oriented

An *action-oriented* goal is a statement that involves an activity, a performance, an operation, or something that produces results. Action verbs describe the type of activity to be performed. Here are some examples of action verbs:

Evaluate	**Investigate**
Appraise	**Influence**
Inform	**restrict**

For example, in the statement "increase the data-entry output," the verb "increase" indicates that the expected result is to raise the productivity from the existing level to a more desirable level. (See the Appendix for a list of other common action verbs.)

What are some other action verbs common to your business or industry that aren't included in the preceding list? Write them here.

S.M.A.R.T. Goals Are Realistic

Realistic goals are practical, achievable, and possible. Goals must motivate people to improve and to reach for attainable ends. For a goal to be motivational, the goal seeker must feel that the goal can be achieved ("I can do it!"). This realization must occur before a person applies effort and energy toward reaching the goal.

Consider this example:

Increase the staff output to 40 completed orders per day.

This is likely to be achievable (realistic) only if the current output is 20-30 orders per day. If the current output is only four, then "40 completed orders per day" might not be realistic with the existing staff. Impossible goals demotivate people and defeat the goal-setting process. No one will strive for a goal that can't be reached. It's important to keep in mind that goals shouldn't be too easy, either. Easy goals aren't any more motivational than unattainable goals are.

Realistic goals strike a balance between what's hard and what's easy to achieve. They require a stretch and may involve added risk in order to reach beyond what's easily achieved. It's that little extra push that makes people progress and improve. Stretching creates the effort required to increase the probability of achieving the goal.

A goal can be practical only if a need exists to achieve it. For example, if there are no more than 10 orders that need to be entered each day, setting a 40-order goal is unnecessary.

It's worthwhile to get feedback from someone who knows you well enough to tell you honestly if you're up to a specific challenge and if your prospective goal is realistic.

Challenging, Realistic Goals

Challenging, realistic goals motivate and encourage higher levels of performance.

REALISTIC OR UNREALISTIC?

Realistic goals are practical, achievable, and possible. Are the following goal components realistic?

	Realistic	Unrealistic
1. Swim a mile.	❑	❑
2. Swim across the Pacific Ocean.	❑	❑
3. Hold your breath until you faint.	❑	❑
4. Learn to play the piano in one year.	❑	❑

Compare your answers with the author's suggested responses in the Appendix.

S.M.A.R.T. Goals Are Time- and Resource-Constrained

Time- and resource-constrained mean that the time and resources to be expended are scheduled and regulated, that there's a deadline by which the outcome must be achieved, and that there's a limit to the costs of achieving it. People generally put off doing things if no deadline is set, because human nature is to find something else to do that has a higher priority. Time constraints encourage action to get objectives completed.

For example, a time- and resource-constrained goal statement might be:

> *Increase the data-entry output of the staff to 40 completed orders per day by June 30, without adding any new data-entry clerks.*

The precise date provides a deadline, while the phrase "without adding any new data-entry clerks" places a limit on the resources that can be used to achieve the goal.

Time constraints and deadlines must be precise to promote the urgency needed to move toward goal achievement. For example, "by the end of October" is more specific than "toward the end of October." But it isn't as precise as "by 10:00 a.m. on October 31." This deadline leaves no doubt about the deadline by which the goal must be achieved.

Some goals are easily achievable when money and resources are unlimited. We just spend until the goal is reached. For example, one way of achieving the "40 orders per day" goal is to have 40 data-entry clerks available. That assures one clerk for each desired letter. In the real world, however, money and resources are constraints you must consider.

The goal statement must contain resource constraints in order to ensure that the goal embodies a practical cost/benefit relationship.

IDENTIFYING SPECIFIC DEADLINES

Which of the following phrases represent deadlines that are specific and precise?

Specific?

	Yes	No
1. Next week	☐	☐
2. Next Thursday by noon	☐	☐
3. As soon as possible	☐	☐
4. First thing Monday morning	☐	☐
5. Before the close of business today	☐	☐
6. Before the close of business today, at 5:00 P.M. PST	☐	☐
7. December 31, (year)	☐	☐

Write your own *precise* deadlines below.

_____

_____

_____

Compare your answers with the author's suggested responses in the Appendix.

Overview:
Writing S.M.A.R.T. Goal Statements

The S.M.A.R.T. acronym defines qualities inherent in actionable, well-planned, and achievable goals. Here's how it works:

S **Pecific:** Detailed, particular, focused

Increase the data-entry output of the staff...

M **easurable:** Quantifiable; providing a standard for comparison and the means to measure results; limiting

...to 40 completed orders per day.

A **ction-oriented:** Performing, operating, producing results

Increase...completed...

R **ealistic:** Practical, achievable, accurate, possible

(Increase)...from current level (20-30 per day) to 40 completed orders per day.

T **ime- and resource-constrained:** Scheduled, regulated by time, having a finite duration of activity, with limited resources

...by June 30 without adding any new data-entry clerks.

Goal Development and Planning

Divide each difficulty into as many parts as is feasible and necessary to resolve it.

–René Descartes

In this part:

- ▶ Goal development.
- ▶ Creating action plans.
- ▶ Overcoming obstacles to goal achievement.
- ▶ Overview: Goal development and planning.

Goal Development

Goals define destinations that you can reach through the combination of relevant knowledge with dreams and desires. Goals enable you to set a direction for your future actions.

When you're identifying goals, it's not important to establish all the detailed elements of those goals or to determine the exact objectives needed to achieve them. The purpose of goal identification is to determine where you want to be in one, two, or more years. The idea is to give substance to what would otherwise be only dreams and desires.

A goal is meant to focus attention on an ultimate destination. Objectives or milestones are only interim steps toward the goal. The specific objectives may change as progress toward the goal is made, but the goal itself, once established, should remain unchanged.

For example, if your mission is to experience many different cultures, and you therefore have a goal to travel around the world, then the various destinations (objectives) might change because of travel constraints or your desire to see places not within the original itinerary or budget. But the original goal—to travel around the world—will not change.

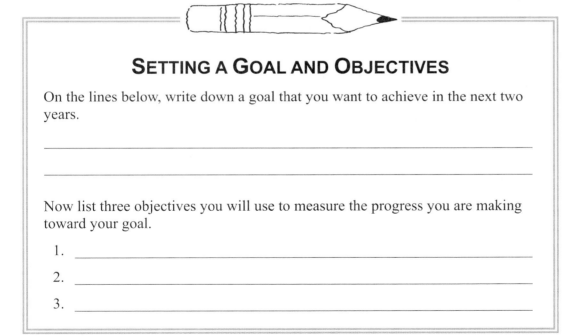

SETTING A GOAL AND OBJECTIVES

On the lines below, write down a goal that you want to achieve in the next two years.

_____

_____

Now list three objectives you will use to measure the progress you are making toward your goal.

1. _____

2. _____

3. _____

Identifying goal opportunities and creating S.M.A.R.T. goal statements (as discussed in Part 2) always precede the task of goal development. Goal development expands goal statements to provide context and substance for expected results and benefits. Identifying opportunities and writing goal statements could result in one, two, 10, or even 50 legitimate goals that require development before work toward goal achievement can begin.

You should fully develop every legitimate goal statement you create. There are five steps to effective goal development:

1. **Classify** goals by type.

2. **Prioritize** within each type.

3. **Establish** standards for performance.

4. **Determine** W.I.I.F.M. (What's In It For Me?).

5. **Visualize** achieving your goals.

Each of these points is very important and necessary to goal development.

Step 1: Classify Goals by Type

The classification of goals requires a review of each goal statement to determine whether its outcome is:

▶ **Essential**: Required for the operation of the business or for personal improvement; it must be done.

▶ **Problem-solving**: Proposes a more appropriate or desired condition or ways around obstacles.

▶ **Innovative**: An activity that will result in something better, faster, cheaper, easier, or safer.

To classify your goals, create a list of goal statements for each goal type. This provides a workable list of identified goals to be achieved.

Essential goals	Essential Goal A
	Essential Goal B
	Essential Goal C, etc.
Problem-solving goals	Problem-solving goal A
	Problem-solving goal B
	Problem-solving goal C, etc.
Innovative goals	Innovative goal A
	Innovative goal B
	Innovative goal C, etc.

Goal statements can sometimes be classified by multiple types. Consider the following goal statement:

> *Learn the French language with sufficient fluency to be able to carry on a complete conversation with a fluent friend and to be able to translate the French instructional materials received with the machinery used in the production plant.*

This innovative goal of learning French to better yourself takes on a problem-solving purpose in the context of its benefit to your company. One motive is pure self-improvement, but accomplishing the goal would also solve a business problem. When this occurs, you should classify the goal by the highest level of need.

Goal Type	Level of Need
Essential	Must be done
Problem-solving	Ought to be done
Innovative	Nice if it could be done

For example, a goal that is both essential and problem-solving should be classified as essential because it must be done; it has the highest level of need. Likewise, a goal that is both essential and innovative should be classified as essential. A goal that is both problem-solving and innovative should be considered problem-solving, because problem-solving goals are more critical than innovative ones.

Step 2: Prioritize Goals within Type

The next step in goal development is to determine the priority of the goals within each type. Setting priorities ensures that you act upon the most important goal first. Prioritize the essential goals first, then the problem-solving goals, and finally the innovative goals, as illustrated below:

Goal Type	Assigned Priority
Essential goals	Essential goal A
	Essential goal B
	Essential goal C, etc.
Problem-solving goals	Problem-solving goal A
	Problem-solving goal B
	Problem-solving goal C, etc.
Innovative goals	Innovative goal A
	Innovative goal B
	Innovative goal C, etc.

Here are some criteria for setting priorities:

▶ **Relative importance**: The achievement of one goal is objectively more important than the achievement of another.

▶ **Time sequence**: If goals A and C can't be achieved until goal B is completed, goal B must have the highest priority.

▶ **Cost-benefit relationship**: If goal B can be achieved at a lower cost than either A or C and will produce immediate benefits, then B should have the highest priority.

Other objective criteria can be used, as well, to establish priorities within goal types. The key is to establish criteria within each type. Remember, however, that type takes precedence; *all* essential goals have higher priority than *any* problem-solving goals, and *all* problem-solving goals have higher priority than *any* innovative goals.

If a problem-solving (ought-to-be-done) goal appears to warrant a priority higher than an essential (must-be-done) goal, then you've probably classified one of them incorrectly. Carefully review each goal statement to ensure that you have assigned the correct classifications.

Prioritization is simpler when you have very specific goal statements. Specific goal statements include *what* is to be accomplished and *why*, along with the expected beneficial results and the cost and resource constraints involved. This information provides everything you need to make a sound judgment on the classification and priority of a goal.

Step 3: Establish Standards for Performance

The next step in goal development is to identify standards for performance that provide measures for the achievement of the goals. These standards serve three purposes:

▶ Indicate progress made toward the goal.

▶ Isolate what remains to be done.

▶ Tell when the goal has been achieved.

These standards must be established before work begins, as they represent specific objectives or milestones to be reached. Proper standards include both a time element (for example, "within three months") and a quantifiable standard for progress (for example, "24 orders per day"). Be sure that your standards are realistic and in line with the overall mission, as well as other goals and objectives.

You should establish three separate standards for your goals:

▶ **Minimal**: Indicates some progress has been made toward the goal, but perhaps not at a pace sufficient to guarantee goal achievement.

▶ **Acceptable**: Progress made is consistent with goal achievement during the time allotted.

▶ **Outstanding**: More progress than expected was achieved when measured at the milestone date. (This level of achievement may require rewards for motivation to balance the risk involved.)

For example, consider this goal:

Increase staff data-entry output from 24 orders completed per day to 40 per day by October 31.

Then you might set the following standards:

▶ **Minimal**: 26 orders completed within 3 months.

▶ **Acceptable**: 31 orders completed within 3 months.

▶ **Outstanding**: 34 orders completed within 3 months.

Standards of performance will indicate progress by specifying when improvement is expected, as well as what the situation will be after goal achievement.

Step 4: Determine W.I.I.F.M. (What's In It For Me?)

Obstacles to goal achievement can result in initial failure, total frustration, or premature abandonment of the goal. This happens because interest alone is never enough to ensure that you reach your goal. Goal achievement requires actions, commitment, and a willingness to persist in an often difficult pursuit.

The value of goal ownership is that it creates motivation and commitment. Commitment, however, is very personal. You're more committed to achieving goals you help create, but you're even more committed to goals that benefit you personally.

Therefore, to achieve your goals, you must determine:

▶ **W.I.I.F.M.** What's in it for me?

▶ **Personal benefit.** How do I directly benefit from achieving this goal?

▶ **Other positive outcomes.** What are other positive outcomes from achieving this goal?

While monetary incentives, recognition, pride, and self-empowerment are all good motivators, you're more committed and perform at your best when you clearly identify the personal benefits of achieving a goal. Here are examples of two goals, one personal and one professional, and how each might benefit you:

Goal	W.I.I.F.M.
Lose 10 pounds off current weight.	*I'll get to wear all those clothes that don't fit now, saving the expense of buying new ones.*
Learn new software package	*I'll be able to do my work more quickly, making me more promotable.*

Commitment to goal achievement sometimes means looking at the goal from a more selfish perspective.

Step 5: Visualize Achieving Your Goals

VISUALIZE: *to form a mental vision, image, or picture (something not visible, or present to sight, or of an abstraction); to make visible to the mind or imagination.*"

–The Oxford English Dictionary, 1989

A powerful tool for goal achievement and success can be the self-confidence you build through *visualization*. Visualization focuses and magnifies the motivational power of the W.I.I.F.M. reward.

When you visualize (imagine), as vividly as possible, the feelings, sensations, moods, and elation that accompany achieving your goal, you use the power of your active imagination to create positive energy toward the result. This happens because the brain can't really differentiate between fantasy and reality. Think about how real a dream can feel upon waking. When you dream or visualize, the brain moves your mind and body toward what it's dreaming or visualizing. Visualization is really "active dreaming" that makes direct and deliberate contact with our subconscious mind.

Studies have suggested a strong relationship between visualization and execution. Many Olympic athletes, NASA astronauts, professional golfers, performance artists (singers, dancers, actors), and baseball and basketball players use repetitive visualization techniques to improve their performance.

The reason repetitive visualization works so well is that it builds:

▶ **Confidence**: Visualizing a task over and over helps you to fully understand the detailed structure of the task's execution. The more we know about something, the more confident we are that we can execute it proficiently and handle any unexpected crises that might arise.

▶ **Comfort**: When you know a task well or have "practiced" it often, you develop a comfort level that puts you at ease. Less stress means more focus and helps to move you more easily toward a successful outcome.

▶ **Correctness**: Visualization is seeing perfection, an ideal state, or flawless execution. You see how it will be when everything goes exactly right and without errors. Repetitive visualizing of these perfect images tells your subconscious how to do it right when the real task is performed.

Research has shown that the brain produces the exact same chemical reactions during visualization that are present while a task is performed. Visualization, therefore, provides you with as many "dress rehearsals" as you need to ensure that your mind knows what to do when the real action starts.

To produce the strongest, most lasting effects, you should incorporate as many of your senses as possible into your visualization. Therefore, visualize in brilliant Technicolor and with full sound effects to experience, for example, what it feels like to:

➤ Listen to someone praise and describe your accomplishments.

➤ Stand on the podium to accept an award for your work.

➤ Write out the deposit slip for the bonus check you earned.

➤ Experience a sigh of relief at the turning point in an important project.

Visualization Process Guidelines

Some visualization process guidelines include:

➤ Set aside the time necessary, and find a quiet place to visualize the positive benefits of achieving your goals.

➤ Visualize with full emotions and feelings.

➤ Be structured and disciplined in your visualization exercises.

➤ Recognize that, even with visualization, the achievement of most goals requires time and commitment; immediate results are *not* the norm.

Visualization is an important tool because, when used properly, your repetitive positive thoughts move you toward taking the actions necessary to achieve your goals. Through visualization, you pay attention to positive images of successful results. These images can encourage and reinforce your beliefs, opinions, and assessments of what you're truly capable of achieving in all areas of your life.

Action Plans

"Let's try an interim goal before we set out
to 'conquer the known world'."

An *action plan* details the activities and actions necessary to accomplish a goal. It's a complete, clear, and realistic document that serves as the foundation for moving forward toward your goal. Action plans organize your thoughts into logical and executable action items. They also document the objectives that underlie the goal and the tactics you will use to achieve it. A written action plan also provides an opportunity for a final review of your documented goals.

With a workable action plan, you're much more likely to achieve your goal. A thorough action plan must answer the following questions:

▶ Is the goal complementary to the mission? Will it achieve the overall purpose?

▶ Is the goal realistic? Is it practical, achievable, and possible?

▶ Did those responsible for achieving the goal participate in its creation?

▶ Have outcomes been quantified so that progress can be measured? This should include both how much progress is expected and by when it's expected to be complete.

▶ Are specific objectives defined for reaching the goal?

▶ Are sufficient resources committed for reaching the goal? Resources should include the required people, funding, equipment, commitment, and anything else you can think of.

▶ Do I have the skills, knowledge, and information needed to achieve this goal? If not, how and where can I gather what I need?

▶ What are the obstacles to goal achievement? What are the contingency plans, if any?

▶ Are the assumptions behind the goal and the steps toward its achievement valid?

The answers to these questions should come out of the goal-setting process.

The purpose of a goal action plan is to provide order and organization. A completed goal action form, which we'll discuss next, provides a roadmap to goal accomplishment.

Goal Action Form

When you're reasonably sure that all or most of the necessary goal details have been defined, the next step is to complete a *goal action form*. The completed form documents your action plan for achieving the goal and acts as a checklist. The form can also be used during periodic reviews to measure progress (plan vs. actual).

GOAL ACTION FORM

Goal:	Rationale for this Goal:

Planned Activities: (Steps, Procedures, Assignments)   Deadlines:

    1. _____   _____

    2. _____   _____

    3. _____   _____

    4. _____   _____

Projected Results (Success Indicators)

❑ Immediate: _____

_____

_____

❑ Long-Term: _____

_____

_____

Obstacles/Constraints: _____

_____

_____

Costs (Dollars, Time, Resources): _____

_____

_____

Person(s) Responsible: _____	Completion Date: _____

You should be able to get all the information you need to complete the goal action form during opportunity identification, documentation, and development. Here's the information required:

Goal

Enter the goal statement in this section. Be sure that the statement conforms to the S.M.A.R.T. method: specific, measurable, action-oriented, realistic, and time- and resource-constrained.

Rationale for this Goal

Describe the importance of the goal to the overall mission. Specify here whether the goal type is essential, problem-solving, or innovative. The rationale should also include the W.I.I.F.M. identified during goal development.

Planned Activities (Steps/Procedures/Assignments)

List the specific objectives that must be met. This is the most important aspect of the action plan, because it provides the measurable steps along the path to the goal, as well as the tactics you'll use to achieve it.

Deadlines

Precise deadlines encourage action and help to establish the priority of the objectives.

Projected Results (Success Indicators or Standards for Performance)

List long- and short-term results that will indicate progress toward or completion of the objectives and the goal. These quantifiable elements provide a standard for comparison and milestones for measuring progress.

Obstacles/Constraints

List the obstacles that could block progress. Detail your contingency plan and the tactics necessary to overcome these obstacles on an *Obstacles Worksheet* (see Obstacles Worksheet in the Appendix).

Cost (Dollars, Time, Resources)

State the allowable expense for achieving the goal in dollars and resources to be used. Cost and resource constraints ensure that the goal will provide an acceptable return on investment.

Person Responsible

Identify who's responsible for achieving the goal. Many individuals may participate in achieving specific objectives, but only one individual can be held accountable for the goal's ultimate achievement.

Completion Date

State the exact date and time by which the goal is to be completed. This information is part of a properly constructed goal statement.

The completed Goal Action Form organizes the various elements of the goal into an orderly, workable roadmap. It provides a reminder of all the actions, activities, expected results, timing, benefits, responsibilities, and contingencies of a well-planned goal.

Obstacles to Goal Achievement

You' will encounter obstacles while trying to reach your goals. These obstacles might be physical, conditional, or psychological. Each type of obstacle is a real barrier to goal achievement. It makes no difference if the barrier is tangible (physical or conditional) or solely in your mind (psychological)—the barrier is real. Therefore, it's very important to:

1. Identify the obstacle

2. Plan a way to overcome the obstacle

Often there are many obstacles to a particular goal. First, you have to identify all conceivable obstacles in order to develop a comprehensive plan for overcoming them.

Common Obstacles

In general, the most common and most dangerous obstacles to goal achievement are:

▶ Procrastination

▶ Unproductive activities

▶ Impatience

Procrastination

Procrastination is putting off work you can do now until later. Waiting for the right time to change jobs, until your children are older to go back to school, and for the perfect moment to approach the boss with a new idea are all examples of procrastination. Conditions might never be perfect. You can always find an excuse to procrastinate. Avoid this temptation; the most perfect time is *right now*!

Procrastination results in inactivity when you think a task is too big, too difficult, too costly, or too risky. To combat inactivity, list the steps you need to follow to reach each planned objective. Then, break down these steps into even smaller steps that set out very specific, simple actions that you know you can complete.

Question: How do you eat an elephant?

Answer: One bite at a time!

The longer you procrastinate, the more pressure you'll feel as the goal's deadline approaches. Pressure often encourages you to take shortcuts. Avoid procrastination by:

▶ Having sufficient motivation to achieve the goal.

▶ Establishing clear priorities for identified tasks.

▶ Breaking needed tasks down into smaller steps.

▶ Setting interim deadlines for each task.

▶ Rewarding yourself when tasks are completed. (It's all about motivation!)

Unproductive Activities

Another common obstacle—and a more dangerous one—to goal achievement is getting sidetracked by unproductive activities. It can be hard to notice such obstacles when there's a lot of activity going on. The problem arises whenever you work on tasks that are unproductive or counterproductive to goal achievement. You're doing things, but *not the right things*.

Doing the right things means performing activities that contribute to goal achievement, that is, the specific objectives identified in the planning process. Simply doing a task in order to be doing something might give the appearance of working toward your goal. However, unless that task contributes directly to goal achievement, the time and resources you invest in it are wasted.

Here are some ways to avoid performing unproductive activities:

▶ Establish clear, focused goal statements.

▶ Perform only those tasks that move you closer to goal achievement.

▶ Review continually the goal plans, priorities, and results.

▶ Keep your eyes on the prize to provide motivation.

Impatience

It's a fact of life that some things just take longer to complete than others. Put a cake in the oven, and no matter how long you stare at the oven, the cake won't bake any faster. You can poke it, prick it, even take it out early, but that won't speed up the process.

Goals are the same way. You can't wait to see positive results, and find yourself impatient:

▶ To see planned steps executed.

▶ For the right resources to become available.

▶ To acquire the knowledge and experience to understand the situation fully.

You want results *now*!

Impatience is a formidable obstacle, because it not only short-circuits progress toward goal achievement, but it also causes you to doubt yourself, your capacity to plan, and your willingness to execute. Combat impatience by refocusing on goal achievement and by reviewing your plan to regain confidence in it. Accomplishing the steps should take as long as you've planned (plus or minus a small amount of time).

If you've created clear goal statements, outlined specific objectives, broken objectives into manageable steps, established necessary goal prerequisites, and delineated appropriate timelines, then just follow through on the plan. Practice patience and stay the course you've plotted. There's a reason people say, "Patience is a virtue." Having patience leads to virtuous results!

Overview:
Goal Development and Planning

In this part, you learned about developing goals, creating action plans, and overcoming obstacles:

▶ There are five steps to effective goal development:

1. **Classify** goals by type.

2. **Prioritize** within each type.

3. **Establish** standards for performance.

4. **Determine** W.I.I.F.M. (What's In It For Me?).

5. **Visualize** achieving your goals.

▶ An **action plan** is a complete, clear, and realistic document that serves as the foundation for moving forward toward your goal. Action plans organize your thoughts into logical and executable action items. They also document the objectives that underlie the goal and the tactics you'll used to achieve it. With a workable action plan, you're much more likely to achieve your goal.

▶ You'll encounter **obstacles** while trying to reach your goals. These obstacles might be physical, conditional, or psychological. It's important to **identify** the obstacle and then plan a way to **overcome** it. **Procrastination**, **unproductive activities**, and **impatience** are three of the most common types of obstacles you'll encounter.

P A R T 5

Goal Achievement

66 *The goal will not be reached if the right distance not be travelled.*"

–Tibetan Proverb

In this part:

- ▶ Taking action on your plan.
- ▶ Overview: Your comprehensive goal foundation.

Taking Action

Identifying opportunities and writing goal statements lay the foundation. Developing goals and formulating action plans provide a roadmap. All of this process sets the stage for success.

Goals are actually *achieved* only through actions and activities. Good planning can tell you how and where to go—but it won't help you succeed without *action*. There are three types of action you have to take to achieve you goals:

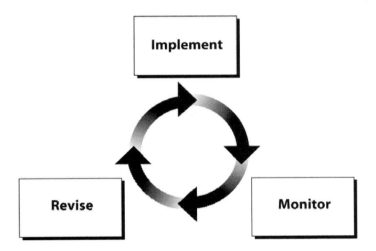

1. **Implement the plan**: Take action on the goals, objectives, and tasks.

2. **Monitor progress**: At specific intervals, check the actions you've taken and the results you've achieved.

3. **Revise objectives**: As necessary, change objectives and tactics to overcome obstacles.

These three types of action create a self-correcting loop that will lead to achieving you goal.

Implementing the Plan

Planning is a good start. The real work, however, begins with taking action to implement new ideas, procedures, policies, and programs. It's easier to take action when you've completed a Goal Action Form, because it specifies *who, what, when, how,* and *how much* for each goal:

▶ **Who** is responsible for coordinating activities?

▶ **What** is to be accomplished?

▶ **When** will the activities be completed?

▶ **How** will the goal be achieved and what obstacles might you encounter?

▶ **How much** is the cost in dollars, resources, and labor to be expended?

Answering these questions is necessary before you can reach your goal. However, only real actions and activities will get you all the way there.

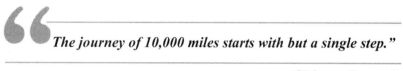

The journey of 10,000 miles starts with but a single step."

–Chinese Proverb

Monitoring Progress

Achieving goals requires that you regularly monitor the actions being taken and measure the results of these actions. Monitoring tells you whether time and effort are producing the results you want. Also, monitoring actions and progress enables you to see which tactics work best, as well as any changes you might need to make to get back on track.

The *Activity/Result Monitoring Worksheet* (see Appendix Part 5), is a helpful tool for doing periodic checks on progress. Here's an overview of the information that should be included:

▶ **Activity**: Information taken from the Planned Activities, Deadlines, and Projected Results sections of a Goal Action Form.

▶ **Relationship to goal and mission**: A list of the complementary relationships that exist among objectives, goals, and mission.

▶ **Expected outcome**: The purpose of the measurable standards of performance established in the goal statement and goal development phases.

▶ **Completion date**: The milestones (dates) set for review of the progress made. It's important to set milestones at practical and planned intervals. They should be clear and precise calendar dates.

▶ **Actual result**: The current status of the activity at the time of monitoring. This is very important, because it tells you whether midcourse adjustments are necessary.

▶ **Revisions to be made**: Any revisions you need to make to your plan based on the progress to date.

If specific results aren't achieved within the specified time period, it's important to diagnose why. Analyze what went wrong before revising objectives. This will help you to avoid making the same mistakes again. Ask yourself:

▶ Were skills, knowledge, or information lacking?

▶ Could I have reached the objective with more/better resources/tools?

▶ Was the goal or objective unrealistic in some way?

▶ Did I work hard enough to achieve the goal or objective?

If adjustments need to be made, include them in the "Revisions to be made" section. These modifications then become new activities in the next round of implementing, monitoring, and revising the goal achievement.

Remember Your Reward

If you achieve the expected result, it's time to reward yourself for a job well done! It's very important to reward yourself continually when you achieve your goals within established guidelines.

Revising Objectives

"Upgrading the workstations is a great goal, but let's go for more."

To achieve your goals, you sometimes have to revise your objectives and tactics. The actions you plan don't always produce exactly the results you want. Sometimes results fall short of planned expectations.

Part of goal development is to identify potential obstacles and ways to overcome them. Even with contingency planning, unforeseen obstacles will occur, requiring you to change direction in order to reach the goal. It might be vitally important to revise your objectives and tactics.

Even so, it's important to remember that the goals themselves shouldn't change. The goal is important, or it wouldn't have made it this far in the process. The monitoring activity will identify the most effective changes to tactics in order to reach your original goal.

Circumstances change, so you should review and revise your Goal Action Form at regular intervals. Review short-term goal plans daily, weekly, or monthly. Review your long-term goals at least once every three months. This creates a useful and dynamic work plan for accomplishing your goals.

Overview: Comprehensive Goal Foundation

It all comes down to planning and then achievement.

Goal-planning activities

Start with your goal-planning activities:

1. Identify goal opportunities.

2. Write S.M.A.R.T. goal statements.

3. Complete goal development.

4. Write an action plan.

Goal Achievement Activities

Then move on to goal achievement:

1. Implement the plan.

2. Monitor results.

3. Revise objectives.

The cycle of implementation, monitoring, and revision should be continual until you achieve your goal. When you revise your objectives and tactics, you then have to implement new plans. This implementation will require new monitoring activities at scheduled intervals. Those activities, in turn, will suggest further revisions, and so on, until each goal is achieved.

When You Achieve Your Goal

When you achieve your goal, reward yourself for a job well done. Go back to your visualization: Did the goal bring what you'd hoped? What new goals do you want to set now? Success in reaching your goals will build confidence as you set new ones. The only limit is your own desire.

APPENDIX

Goals and Goal Setting Process

What Is a Goal?

A goal is a specific and measurable accomplishment to be achieved within time and cost constraints. Goals are written statements of intent and results to be achieved. Such statements contain:

- ▶ Action verbs.
- ▶ Measurable outcomes.
- ▶ Specific dates for accomplishment.
- ▶ Cost and resource constraints.

Mission statements define your cause and provide direction for goals.

Objectives are the tactics you use to achieve goals. They must be complementary to the goal and the mission.

Why Set Goals?

Well-defined goals enable people to design and implement strategies in their life and work objectives to achieve a mission.

Goals will:

- ▶ Establish direction.
- ▶ Identify results.
- ▶ Improve teamwork.
- ▶ Heighten performance.

Who Sets Goals?

The parties involved in achieving the goal should help define it. People are more committed to achieving goals that they helped create.

How Are Goals Set?

Creating goals is a four-task process:

1. Identify opportunities for goals based on:

    ▷ Needs

    ▷ Roles

    ▷ Responsibilities

2. Write S.M.A.R.T. goal statements:

    ▷ **S**pecific: Detailed, particular, focused.

    ▷ **M**easurable: Quantifiable, limiting.

    ▷ **A**ction-oriented: That produce results.

    ▷ **R**ealistic: Practical, achievable.

    ▷ **T**ime- and resource-constrained: Scheduled, regulated by time and deadlines.

3. Develop goals:

    a. Classify goals by type.

    b. Prioritize within each type.

    c. Establish standards for performance.

    d. Determine W.I.I.F.M. ("What's in it for me?").

    e. Visualize the sights, sounds, and feelings of goal achievement.

4. Formulate action plans:

    a. Use the Goal Action Form as a roadmap to goal achievement

    b. Identify obstacles to goal achievement

How Are Goals Achieved?

Goal achievement requires you to:

1. Implement the plan.

2. Monitor progress:

    a. Measure planned vs. actual results.

    b. Determine which elements work and which don't work.

    c. Understand *why* they worked or didn't work.

3. Revise objectives:

    a. Change tactics, not goals.

    b. Apply what works.

4. Restart the cycle:

    a. Implement the plan.

    b. Monitor progress.

    c. Revise objectives.

Continue until your goal is achieved. *Success!*

Appendix to Part 1

Comments & Suggested Responses

Identify the Goal Elements

1. **Action verb:** gain

   Measurable outcome: five new customers, gross sales of $20,000

   Specific date: July 1

   Cost constraint: within expense budget of $1,000

2. **Action verb:** expand

   Measurable outcome: market share of 5%

   Specific date: December 31

   Cost constraint: without increasing advertising expense

3. **Action verb:** secure

   Measurable outcome: two new clients, $30,000 income

   Specific date: June 30

   Cost constraint: no more than 30% of time to service

Appendix to Part 3

Comments & Suggested Responses

How Specific Is the Goal?

Statements 1, 4, and 7 are **too general.** They state only broad intents for action.

Statements 2, 5, and 8 are a little more specific, but **not specific enough** to be used in goal statements.

Statements 3, 6, and 9 are **more specific** and focus intent on a desired outcome.

Which Are Measurable Outcomes?

1. No, because the outcome can't be quantified. *Better* is a relative term and no indication is given as to what *better service* will mean for each specific customer.

2. Yes, *five work days* is a measurable outcome. It can be determined whether every letter was answered within five days after it was received.

3. No. *Significantly* is too ambiguous a term for goals. It's relative to an undefined standard.

4. Yes. *Fifty percent of current levels* is measurable, assuming that the number of complaints currently being received is known.

5. No, because *very productive* isn't measurable or quantifiable.

Action Verbs

A list of common action verbs is shown below. Place an **X** next to the words that may be commonly used by you and those around you.

activate	construct	gain	learn	qualify
add	determine	implement	make	quantify
answer	document	improve	monitor	research
appraise	develop	increase	match	review
authorize	define	invest	negotiate	revise
change	expand	investigate	purchase	restrict
correct	enroll	incorporate	provide	reduce

create	evaluate	influence	produce	select
classify	establish	interview	prioritize	secure
complete	forecast	identify	process	sign up
clarify	formulate	introduce	plan	support

Realistic or Unrealistic?

Whether a goal is realistic or not, of course, depends on the people and circumstances involved. But based on certain assumptions and generalities, here are the author's responses to these goals.

1. Realistic. Swimming a mile has been accomplished by many individuals. With practice, many people could achieve this goal.

2. Unrealistic. Swimming across the Pacific Ocean is impossible, even for expert swimmers.

3. Unrealistic. Although holding your breath until you faint is possible, the author's opinion is that it's impractical and therefore unrealistic. If there were a legitimate purpose for holding your breath until you faint, then perhaps this activity could be classified as realistic.

4. Realistic. Learning to play the piano is achievable, although learning in a year, depending upon what you want to play, might be difficult.

Identify the Specific Deadlines

Statements 2, 6, and 7 are specific enough.

Statements 1 and 3 are too general.

Statements 4 and 5 at first appear to be specific, but the phrases "first thing" and "close of business" might be interpreted differently by different people. Deadlines for goals must leave no room for interpretation.

Appendix to Part 4

OBSTACLES WORKSHEET

Some obstacles to goal achievement that are expected, probable, or likely to occur are:

Obstacle: _____

_____

Solution: _____

_____

Actions to implement solutions: _____

_____

_____

Obstacle: _____

_____

Solution: _____

_____

Actions to implement solutions: _____

_____

_____

Obstacle: _____

_____

Solution: _____

_____

Actions to implement solutions: _____

_____

_____

Appendix to Part 5

ACTIVITY/RESULT MONITORING WORKSHEET

Date: _____

Goal statement: _____

_____

_____

Activity: _____

_____

Relationship to goal and mission: _____

_____

Expected outcome: _____

_____

Completion date: _____

Actual Result: _____

_____

Revisions to be made: _____

_____

Additional Reading

Crisp 50-Minute Series books:

Haynes, Marion E. *Project Management.*

Karlson, David, Ph.D. *Marketing Your Consulting or Professional Services.*

Scott, Cynthia D., M.P.H., Ph.D. and Dennis T. Jaffe, Ph.D. and Glenn R. Tobe, M.A. *Organizational Vision, Values, and Mission.*

Riley, Lorna. *Achieving Results.*

Other related reading:

Cairo, Jim. *Motivation and Goal Setting.* Hawthorne, NJ: Career Press, 1993.

Coonradt, Charles A., with Lee Nelson. *The Game of Work.* Salt Lake City, UT: Shadow Mountain, 1993.

Covey, Steven, Ph.D. *First Things First.* New York, NY: Simon & Schuster, 1994.

Covey, Steven, Ph.D. *The Seven Habits of Highly Effective People.* New York, NY: Simon & Schuster, 1988.

Freeman, Arthur, Ph.D. and Rose DeWolf. *The 10 Dumbest Mistakes Smart People Make.* New York, NY: HarperCollins Publishers, Inc., 1992.

Jones, Elizabeth F. *You Can Get There From Here.* Nags Head, NC: Washington Publications, Inc., 1990.

Klauser, Henriette Anne, Ph.D. *Write It Down, Make It Happen.* New York, NY: Scribner, 2000.

Waitley, Dennis. *The New Dynamics of Goal Setting.* New York, NY: William Morrow and Company, Inc., 1996.

Wilson, Susan B. *Goal Setting.* New York, NY: AMACOM, 1994.

50-Minute™ Series

If you enjoyed this book, we have great news for you.
There are more than 200 books available in the
Crisp Fifty-Minute™ Series.

Subject Areas Include:

Management and Leadership
Human Resources
Communication Skills
Personal Development
Sales and Marketing
Accounting and Finance
Coaching and Mentoring
Customer Service/Quality
Small Business and Entrepreneurship
Writing and Editing

For more information visit us online at

www.CrispSeries.com